Warm & fuzzy

The most *adorable* animal pictures ever

First distributed in 1995 in the
United States of America by
Reading's Fun Ltd
119 South Main Street
Fairfield, IA 52556

Produced by Weldon Russell Pty Ltd
107 Union Street
North Sydney
NSW 2060, Australia

A member of the Weldon International
Group of Companies

Chief Executive: Elaine Russell
Publisher: Karen Hammial
Managing Editor: Ariana Klepac
Editors: Megan Johnston, Kayte Nunn
Caption Writers: Susan Hurley, Jane Sheard
Designers: Silvia Martello, Catherine Martin
Picture Researcher: Anne Ferrier
Production: Dianne Leddy

Printed by Tien Wah Press in Singapore

A KEVIN WELDON PRODUCTION

endpapers: emperor penguins
cover: basset hounds
back cover: baby harp seal
page 1: bears
opposite title page: kittens
opposite: polar bears

Harp Seal: "Snow doubt about it – it's good to be alive."

Sea Otter: Wet behind the ears – you otter be in pictures.

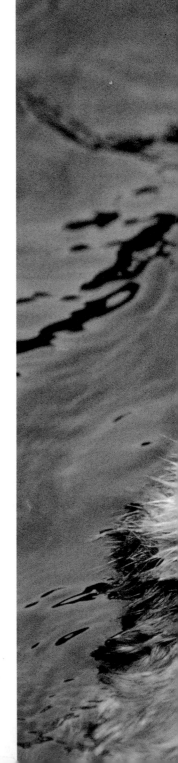

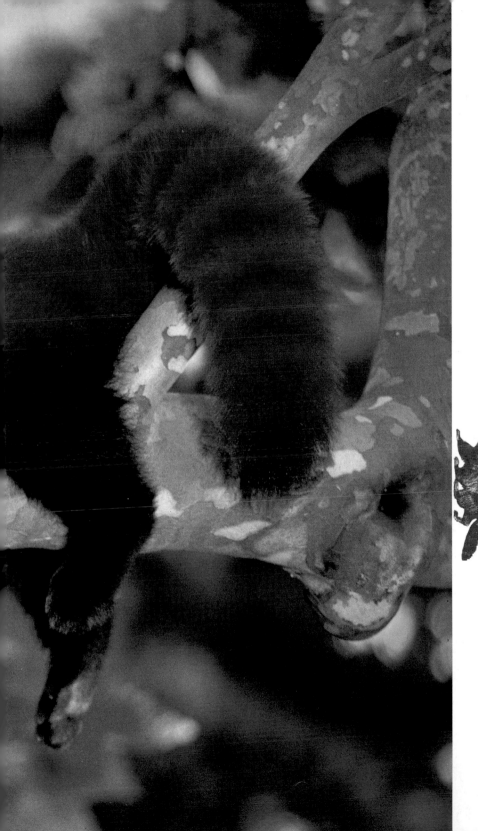

Red Panda:
Branching out on his own.

Porcupines: *"Quill you be my baby?"*

Mountain Goats: *"Here's looking at you, Kid."*

Chimpanzees:
"He ain't hairy; he's my brother."

Hedgehog: Prickly package – handle with care.

Red Squirrel: Tail of one sitting.

Tigers: Stars in stripes.

Cheetahs: Spotted snoozin'.

German Shepherd and Kitten:
Winning by a nose.

 Kitten: White was she born so beautiful?

Harvest Mouse: Clutching at straws.

House Mouse: There's a hole lot going on in here.

Rabbit: A winter's cottontail.

Puma: "I wonder if there's a mountain lyin' over there?"

Red Fox Pup:
Playing safe in
a cubby hole.

Red Fox Pups: Red-necking.

Red Foxes: Learning the fox of life.

Cattle: Moo-oove in a little closer.

Sea Otter: "See? I'm otterly adorable."

Sea Lion: Facing up to the nitty-gritty.

Hippopotamus and Calf:
Big mother's watching you.

Panda: Panda-ring to a wish for sleep.

Yorkshire Piglets: Hamming it up.

Koalas: Love nose no bounds.

Baby Koala: Hanging loose, out on a limb.

 **Black-tailed Prairie Dog:** A furry fine specimen.

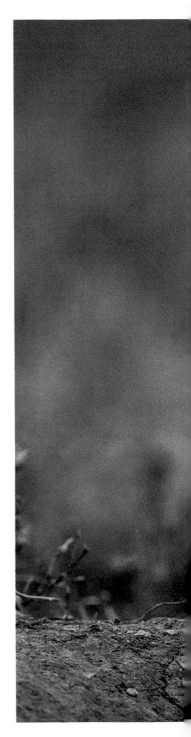

Cocker Spaniel: Puppy love.

Gorillas: A real ape-titude for parenting.

Mountain Gorillas:
Gorillas in the midst of sleep.

Chick and Guinea Pig: It's chickmate.

Piglets: These little pigs stayed home.

Puppy: "Hay! I'm no dog in a manger."

Peccaries: Digging in together.

Wild Boar: Getting to the root of the matter.

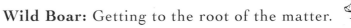

Mute Swan and Cygnets: Snuggled down for a moment of silence.

White Tern Chick: "Is it my tern next?"

Orang-utan: Parental support.

Sumatran Orang-utan:
Son and hair.

Cheetahs: "My mom knocks the spots off other cats."

Caracal and Cub: Bound by the strongest lynx.

Raccoon: Even baby bandits get stuck up.

Raccoon: "I've got my mask, but where's the snorkel?"

African Elephants: Making a trunk call.

African Elephants: Keeping in step with the world.

Dormouse:
Heads or tails, she wins.

Ground Squirrel:
Just looking.

Fox Squirrel: Tum-thing worth seeing.

Canada Geese: Take a gander at this fine family.

Mallard and Ducklings:
Reflected glory.

Baby Porcupine:
"This scent sends tingles down my spines."

Arctic Fox Cub: "I'll be all white in a few months."

Peking Duckling:
"Only four days old
and I'm already making
wise-quacks."

Robin: Getting a handle on life.

Woodchuck: "Me? I didn't throw anything!"

Lioness and Cub: Personal pride.

Lioness and Cub:
Taking things lyin' down.

Golden Retriever Pups:
Leading a dog's life?
It's litter-ally
wonderful.

Dormouse: Finding the answer to life's thorny questions.

Bank Vole: "Hey! I've just had a windfall."

Emperor Penguin: Chubby chicker.

Short-tailed Ermine:
Stoat-ally different in winter camouflage.

Swan: Swan down
and one left in the nest.

Ducklings:
Four snugly ducklings with
a freshly hatched plot.

Martens: "I've branched out on my own…"

"…and I've found a hole new way of life."

Baby Bobcat: "I bet that loopy lupus doesn't know I can lip-read."

Grey Wolf Cubs:
"Sit still. I want to tell you a secret."

Grizzly Bear Cub: Bear-ly three
months old and everything's
falling into place.

Yellow-bellied Marmot: Just popped up to say hello.

Lioness and Cub: "Okay young 'un. I'll soon have you licked into shape."

ion Cub: "At last – something to get my teeth into."

Water Vole: This vole-uptuous little creature just loves picnics by the river.

Kitten: Paws in the middle of a game.

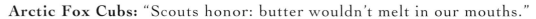

Arctic Fox Cubs: "Scouts honor: butter wouldn't melt in our mouths."

Mallard Duckling: Water big world it is for one so small.

Hamster: "There's something ferny going on around here."

Donkey: This baby doesn't mewl —
she's positively bray-zen!

Rabbits: Head and shoulders above the rest.

 **Zebras:** A heady affair.

Grizzly Bear Cub: Barking up the right tree.

Polar Bears: Cold-comfort charm – gently does it.

Weddell Seals: Mother love sealed with a kiss.

Index

Acknowledgments

Weldon Russell would like to thank the following photographic libraries for supplying pictures for reproduction:

Animals, Animals: p 80 (Annup & Manoj Shah).
Aquila: p 25 (top) (Wayne Laniken); p 26/27 (M. Durham); p 57 (Wayne Laniken); p 69 (Robert Maier); p 66/67 (E. A. Janes).
Ardea: p 20 (Liz & Tony Bomford); p 42/43 (Kenneth W. Fink).
Auscape: endpapers (G. Robertson); p 34 (Jean-Paul Ferrero); p 35 (Jean-Paul Ferrero); p 71 (Grahame Roberts).
Australian Picture Library: p 1 (ZEFA); p 6 (left) (VOLVOX); p 27 (right) (Julie Habel); p 28 (left) (VOLVOX); p 28/29 (right) (VOLVOX); p 36 (ZEFA); p 84 (ZEFA).
Austral International: p 6/7 (FPG/Austral); p 8/9 (Pictor Int/Austral); p 17 (Rex Features); p 32/33 (Pictor/Austral).
Balthis, Frank S.: p 74.
Bentsen, Steve: p 50.
Britstock — IFA: p 12/13 (BCA); p 19 (TPC).
Bruce Coleman: p 14 (William S. Paton); p36/37 (right) (Wayne Laniken); p 43 (right) (Hans Reinhard); p 46 (Alain Compost); p 89 (Hans Reinhard).
Frank Lane Picture Agency: p 4/5 (Silvertris); p 16/17 (Fritz Polking); p 21 (R. Tidman).
Global Pictures: p 59 (Robert E. Barber); p 75 (Joe McDonald).
Horizon: cover p 63 I.F.A; p 94 (left).
The Image Bank: p 25 (Paul McCormick); p 41 (G & M David De Lossy); p 64 (Joe Van Os).

Imagery: p 56 (S. Nielsen).
Kuhn, Dwight R.: p 60/61; p 70.
Leonard Lee Rue III: p 78.
Len Rue Jr.: p 30/31.
McDonald, Joe: p 22.
McDonald, Mary Ann: p 23; p 79.
Nature Photographers Ltd: p 40 (E. A. Janes).
Naturfotograferna/ N Sweden: p 72 (Tore Hagman).
NHPA: p 45 (E. A. Janes); p 49 (Anthony Bannister); p 51 (John Shaw); p 58 (John Shaw); p 68 (Stephen Dalton); p 73 (E. A. Janes); p 86/87 (Eric Soder); p 82/83 (Stephen Dalton).
Oxford Scientific Films: p 38/39 (right) (Andrew Plumptre); p 52 (Richard Packwood); p 53 (Martyn Colbeck); p 54 (bottom) (Daniel J. Fox); p 62 (Richard Packwood); p 90/91 (Paul Taylor).
Peter Arnold Inc.: p 44 (Roland Seitre).
The Photo Library Sydney: p 2/3; p 15 (Rod Planck); p 33 (right) (Andy Sacks); p 88; p 85; p 92 (Johan Elzenga).
Photo Researchers Inc.: p 81 (Gregory G. Dimijian); p 24 (Tom & Pat Leeson).
Planet Earth Pictures: p 10 (D. Robert Franz); p 55 (Cameron Read); p 65 (Roger de la Harpe); p 77 (D. Robert Franz).
Stock Photos: p 18 (The Stock Market); p 54 (The Stock Market).
Survival Anglia: p 48 (Alan Root); p 94/95 (right) (Rick Price).
Tom Stack & Associates: p 11 (Mary Clay); p 41(top) (Inga Spence); p 47 (Brian Parker).
Wildlight/Liaison: p 38 (Kathleen Campbell).
Wildstock: p 76 (Erwin & Peggy Bauer); p 93 (Erwin & Peggy Bauer).